RAILWAYS TO

Actual and

The Late
REGINALD B. FELLOWS
M.A., LL.M of Trinity College, Cambridge
Hon. Canon of Westminster Cathedral

THE OLEANDER PRESS
OF CAMBRIDGE

THE OLEANDER PRESS
17 STANSGATE AVENUE
CAMBRIDGE CB2 2QZ
ENGLAND

ISBN 0 902675 62 1

AUTHOR'S NOTE

The essay presented in the following pages is a completely rewritten and enlarged version of material assembled for various papers I have produced in the last ten years. An account of the railways between London and Cambridge appeared in my London to Cambridge by Train: 1845-1938, *the University Press " New Year " book for* 1939, *of which a limited number was printed for private circulation. The immediate cause of the researches I undertook for that study was the running of an excursion train from King's Cross to Cambridge on* 24 *August* 1938, *using* 1888 *Scotch express stock hauled by Patrick Stirling's " single " engine No.* 1. *This excursion was particularly interesting to me as in August* 1888 *I had watched " the* 10 a.m. *down special express King's Cross to Edinburgh," as it was called in the working notices, pass through Hatfield, near which town I then lived.*

Since 1939 *I have contributed papers on actual and proposed Cambridge railways to the Railway Club, the Cambridge Antiquarian Society, and the Cambridge University Railway Club, and an article to* The Locomotive. *Naturally, much of what I wrote then forms part of this essay, but in preparing it for publication I have revised it throughout.*

I wish to thank Mr. R. Barnard Way for kindly drawing the plan of Cambridge, and also Mr. H. R. Mallett, of the University Library, for his help when I examined the railway plans which are under his care in the map room.

R. B. F.

(*Photo : Locomotive Publishing Co.*)

Great Eastern Railway Locomotive No. 88, designed by Robert Sinclair and built by Schneider at Le Creusot in 1866 : photograph taken at Cambridge in 1870 with Station Staff

ALTHOUGH the railway to Cambridge was not opened until 29 July 1845, there had been several earlier surveys for a railway to that town, most of them being of course for lines from London.

The first survey for a railway in the immediate neighbourhood of Cambridge was made in 1821 by William James and was the subject of a detailed report dated April 1822, sent by him to the Earl of Hardwicke.* The report was headed " Report on an Engine Railroad from Bishop's Stortford to Clayhithe Sluice with a branch to Waddon and an estimate thereof." The railway was proposed in place of a canal for which an Act of Parliament had been obtained for connecting the existing Stortford Navigation with that at Cambridge. James reported as follows :

> " Having carefully surveyed the line selected for the proposed canal . . . and having attentively perused and considered the Act of George III by which the Company is formed to execute this work, I can confidently state that the geological formation of the line of country is admirably adapted to the improved engine railroad system by regular gradients, and that the powers given to the Company are ample for the construction and enjoyment thereof, and the work may immediately commence."

Lord Hardwicke, who had interested himself in getting the Act for the canal, was, however, very doubtful whether the powers given by that Act would be applicable to the substitution of a railway.

The railway as surveyed by William James would have passed through the following parishes in the neighbourhood of Cambridge : Great Shelford, Trumpington, Cherry Hinton, Fen Ditton, and Horningsea. Further surveys were proposed by him for railways from Cambridge

---

* *The Two James's and the Two Stephensons ; or, the Earliest History of Passenger Transit on Railways*, by E.M.S.P. (London, 1861), pp. 32-36. *The Mining Journal*, 26 December 1857, has a reference to the report

to Lincoln and Norwich, and also to Lynn, and Bills for these were to be deposited for the next session of Parliament. No railway was, however, made, and even the construction of the canal was not proceeded with.

In 1825 John and George Rennie, the well-known railway engineers, surveyed a line to run from a terminus below London Bridge and to proceed by the valley of the Lea near Ware and thence through Braughing and Barkway to Cambridge and beyond. An official notice in *The Cambridge Chronicle* of 11 November 1825 stated that a Bill would be deposited for the Session of 1827 for the construction of the railway and that the Company was to be incorporated under the name of the Northern Rail-Road Company. The line was to end at Cromford in Derbyshire and to join the proposed High Peak Railway and thence reach Manchester ; but nothing came of the matter.

During 1834 another survey was made for a railway, or, as described in the *London Gazette* (21 November 1834), for " a railway or tram-road from the City of London to the Town of Cambridge."*

The line was surveyed by Nicholas Wilcox Cundy, the well-known canal engineer, and was to run from London through Bishop's Stortford to Cambridge and eventually to York. Just south of Cambridge a branch to Norwich was proposed. Preliminary steps for a Bill in Parliament were taken, and plans were deposited with the Clerk of the Peace for Cambridgeshire. These plans show that the station at Cambridge was to be on the south side of the Huntingdon Road near the present St. Giles and St. Peter's Cemetery, a good mile and a quarter from Market Hill. The Company was to be incorporated as the Grand Northern & Eastern Railway. Beyond the depositing of plans, nothing was done towards the construction of the railway. The plans, however, with some modifications, were adopted by James Walker, by arrangement with N. W. Cundy, as the line for which the Northern & Eastern Railway deposited their Bill for the Session of 1836.

In the Parliamentary Session of 1836 a Bill was introduced for a line from London to York through Cambridge, surveyed by Joseph Gibbs in the previous year. The line was to run from London by Dunmow and Saffron Walden

---

* In many of the early notices as to the deposit of Bills for Parliament the expression " a railway or tram road " is used.

to Cambridge and York; the station at Cambridge was to be " at the east end of Jesus Green." A branch line was to be made from Saffron Walden or thereabouts to Norwich. The Company was to be called the " Great Northern Railway ".* The Bill for this line was read a first time, but was withdrawn by the promoters on defeat at second reading.

In the same Parliamentary Session a Bill was introduced for another railway from London to Cambridge. This line, based on Cundy's survey of 1834, had been re-surveyed by James Walker in 1835, and his proposals had met with considerable local support. A Public Meeting was held on 23 January 1836 at the Cambridge Town Hall to consider whether support should be given to James Walker's proposed line or to the line, referred to above, surveyed by Joseph Gibbs, and it was agreed that James Walker's line for the Northern & Eastern Railway should be supported, and a committee was appointed to prepare a Petition to Parliament in favour of that Company's Bill.†

The Committee included the Mayor of Cambridge, the Master of Downing College, the President of Queen's College, and one of the Fellows of Trinity College. The Bill was for the incorporation of a company to be called the " Northern & Eastern Railway " for a railway from London to Cambridge, with a branch line from it starting just short of Cambridge in the parish of Trumpington and running on the south-east outskirts of Cambridge through the parish of Cherry Hinton to Newmarket and Thetford, and thence to Norwich and Yarmouth. Three sites were named, as alternatives, for the terminus in London, two being on plots of land between Kingsland Road and Hackney Road, near the junction of those roads in Shoreditch, the third being in Islington on the north side of York Place, City Road, close to the Regent's Canal. The promoters had intended to include in their Bill a railway to Lincoln and York from Cambridge, but the survey was not completed in time.‡ Parliament, however,

---

* This company had no connection with the well-known railway of the same name, which was not incorporated until 1846.

† See *The Cambridge Chronicle*, 12 February 1836, for the Committee's notice of the Petition.

‡ See ,' Report to the Committee for promoting a railway from London to York, with a branch to Norwich, by James Walker, F.R.S.", dated 30 June 1835, and published in full in *The Railway Magazine* of January 1836.

SITES PROPOSED FOR RAILWAY STATIONS AT CAMBRIDGE,
1834-64

No. on Map	Approximate Site			Year of Scheme	Proposed by
1	Huntingdon Road, south side, near present St. Giles and St. Peter's Cemetery			1834	N. W. Cundy, for Grand Northern & Eastern Railway
2	East end of Jesus Green			1836	Joseph Gibbs, for a Company to be called Great Northern Railway (see footnote p. 3)
3	" In the parish of Little St. Mary " (Probably on Coe Fen or the Leys)			1836	Cambridge & Bury St. Edmunds Railway
4	Near present River Farm House at the river end of Latham Road			1836	Northern & Eastern Railway
	ditto			1836	Great Eastern & Western Junction Railway
	ditto			1841	East Anglian Railway
	ditto			1843	Thetford & Cambridge Railway
5	Huntingdon Road, opposite the " Castle remains "			1841	Joseph Gibbs' revised line
6	PRESENT STATION NEAR HILLS ROAD			1844	Eastern Counties Railway (named Great Eastern Railway in 1862) Station opened July 1845 No other station was opened. Other Companies having access to Cambridge used this station
7	" In or near Coe Fen "			1844	Cambridge & Lincoln Railway (original plan)
8	Near Old Town Gaol, now Queen Anne Terrace, as an additional station			1846	Mayor's Committee
9	North end of Sheep's Green, as an additional station			1846	Eastern Counties Railway
10	Botanic Garden, opposite to			1846	Cambridge & Oxford Railway
11	ditto	south side of		1847	Royston & Hitchin Railway
12	ditto	north-east of, bounded by Russell Street and Hills Road		1848	ditto
13	ditto	adjoining Botanic Garden		1850	Cambridge & Shepreth Junction Railway
14	Queen's Road, near Sidgwick Avenue			1846	Cambridge & Oxford Railway
15	Silver Street, at river end			1851	Royston & Hitchin Railway
16	Little St. Mary Lane and Mill Lane, near river end			1846	Cambridge & Oxford Railway
17	Emmanuel Road, where Orchard Street abuts on it			1864	Great Northern Railway

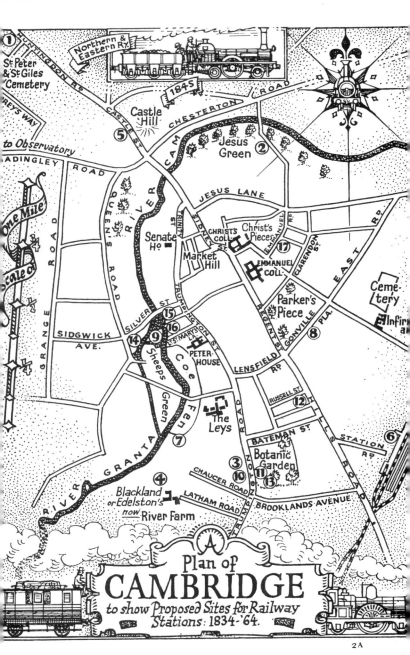

Plan of
CAMBRIDGE
to show Proposed Sites for Railway
Stations: 1834-'64.

cut out of the Bill even the proposed branch to Norwich and Yarmouth and only sanctioned the direct line to Cambridge (just over 53 miles in length). The Bill, thus cut down, received the Royal Assent on 4 July 1836, and it was confidently expected that the railway to Cambridge would be constructed in about three years. The line as authorised ran by way of Tottenham, Broxbourne, Bishop's Stortford, Audley End, and Shelford.

The Act, 6 & 7 William IV, c. ciii, was entitled " An Act for making a railway to form a communication between London and Cambridge with a view to its being extended hereafter to the Northern and Eastern Counties of England." Section 7 fixed the London terminus on the Islington site, and at Cambridge the railway was " to terminate with a Depot on the south side of the river Cam near a certain farm house called Eddleston Farm in the said parish of Trumpington and to communicate with the town of Cambridge by a branch road to join the London and Cambridge turnpike road at or near Leys and Cow Common in the parish of Little St. Mary Cambridge in the county of Cambridge." The station, or " Depot " as it is called in the Act, would have been about 1¼ miles from the centre of Cambridge (Market Hill), and at the river end of the present Latham Road, about 100 yards south of the river Cam or Granta. The farm called in the Act Eddleston Farm* is now known as River Farm. The " branch road " mentioned in the Act was a carriage road to be made by the railway company as an approach to the station and to join the Trumpington Road nearly opposite the present Brooklands Avenue.

---

* The name of this farm also appears as " Edleston's " in contemporary documents.

WHEN the Northern & Eastern Railway got its Act to make its line to Cambridge, it was intended to make Cambridge a centre for railways. Preliminary steps were taken for Bills for four other railways to be made converging on Cambridge :

(i) *The Great Eastern & Western Junction Railway.*

From the station at Cambridge of the Northern & Eastern Railway, this line was to run by Caxton and St. Neots to Bedford and thence to join the London & Birmingham Railway near Stoney Stratford (*i.e.* Bletchley).

(ii) *The Cambridge & Bury St. Edmunds Railway.*

From Cambridge " with a station in the parish of Little St. Mary," then going through Trumpington parish with a branch to the Northern and Eastern Railway from London, and on through Cherry Hinton, Fulbourn, etc., to Bury.

(iii) *The Oxford & Cambridge Railway* (so described in the notice for the Bill).

" To commence at Oxford and to terminate at or near Cambridge passing through Bicester, Buckingham, Stoney Stratford, Newport Pagnel, Bedford and St. Neots, with a branch to Huntingdon."

(iv) *Cambridge Transverse Railway.*

Eastward to Newmarket and Bury St. Edmunds ; westward to St. Ives, Huntingdon, Kettering and Market Harborough (to join proposed South Midland Railway). The site for the station at Cambridge was not mentioned, but the railway was to keep on the northern outskirts of the town, near Barnwell Pool, leaving the Cambridge gas works on the south and crossing the river Cam in the parish of Chesterton and uniting in the most convenient place with the London & Cambridge, or " Walker's line." It was to cross the Ely road by Chesterton causeway, pass over the open fields to Howe House, where it would cross the Huntingdon Turnpike Road, thus keeping clear of the Observatory, and so on to St. Ives.

Official notices of these proposed railways were published in 1836, and three of the lines are shown on the map attached to the Report presented at the first General Meeting of the Northern & Eastern Railway Company held on 5 August 1836, described as " Lines of various railways flowing into the Northern and Eastern line."

But nothing came of these schemes. It soon became clear that want of capital would prevent the Northern & Eastern Company from reaching Cambridge for quite a number of years, and that for the same reason there was no likelihood of that Company's intended extension from Cambridge to York being proceeded with, though the surveys were being completed.

Events proved that this pessimistic forecast was correct. Broxbourne was only reached in 1840, and on 16 May 1842 Bishop's Stortford became the terminus, an Act having been passed in 1840 to enable the company to abandon its powers to construct the line beyond that town. Want of capital also compelled the Company to seek Parliamentary sanction for the substitution of a less costly line in London than that sanctioned under the original Act. The separate terminus at Islington was not proceeded with, nor the line to it from Tottenham, which would have required some heavy tunnelling work. A cheaper line from Tottenham was substituted to join the Eastern Counties Railway at Stratford, and arrangements were made for the Northern & Eastern to have running powers over the line from Stratford with the use of the Eastern Counties' Shoreditch terminus. The Eastern Counties line was laid with a 5-ft. gauge, and this determined the gauge of the Northern & Eastern, though the question of a mixed gauge between Stratford and Shoreditch was considered.

On the Northern & Eastern Company's abandonment of its powers to make the line to Cambridge, an attempt was made by an independent company to continue railway communication from Bishop's Stortford to Cambridge and beyond. A meeting was held in London on 30 December 1840 to promote a Bill for a railway to join the Northern & Eastern line at Bishop's Stortford to run to Cambridge to a terminus near Eddleston's Farm, as in the Act of 1836.* There was to be a branch running from this line

* *The Times*, 1 January 1841 ; see also C. H. Cooper, *Annals of Cambridge*, Vol. IV, p. 632.

just short of Cambridge, keeping to the east of the town, to Newmarket, Thetford, Norwich, and Yarmouth. The line had been surveyed by a well-known railway engineer, John U. Rastrick. At the preliminary meeting in London the Company was to be called " The Norfolk, Suffolk & Cambridge Railway," but the name was altered to " The East Anglian Railway," and under that name plans were deposited and notice was given in *The London Gazette* of 23 February 1841 of intention to apply for an Act in the ensuing Session. In spite of substantial support nothing came of the matter.

Joseph Gibbs' proposal of 1836 for a line from London to York through Cambridge was also revived, though in a modified form, and in the same issue of *The London Gazette* notice was given of intention to apply for an Act to make that railway, commencing in the parish of Clerkenwell and running by way of Ware, Barkway, Cambridge, and Lincoln to a junction with the Great North of England Railway near York. Gibbs' plans showed three methods of reaching Cambridge : (i) a completely new line from Middleton Gardens near " The Angel," Islington, to Cambridge by Ware and Barkway ; (ii) the use from London of the existing Eastern Counties and Northern & Eastern lines from Shoreditch terminus as far as Broxbourne, and then a new line on by Ware ; (iii) the use of the existing line between Tottenham and Broxbourne only, with a new line from Tottenham to a terminus at Islington as in (i) and a new line as in (ii) from Broxbourne to Cambridge. Detailed plans and sections and estimates were prepared for this railway and were published in March 1841 in the Report of the Special Commission appointed by the Board of Trade on Railway communication schemes between London and the North.

Gibbs' proposed site for the station at Cambridge was to the north of the town, nearly opposite the Castle, where the line would pass below the Huntingdon Road. Gibbs stated in his Report that in the 1836 plans before Parliament the railway was shown as passing on the east side of Cambridge but in the plans of 1841 on the western side of the town, to avoid opposition by landowners. It will be remembered that in the 1836 plans the station at Cambridge was shown at the east end of Jesus Green.

Nothing came of the proposed railway scheme of 1841. That year was a particularly bad one financially and, as

Lewin remarks, " the hard times through which the country was now passing were severely felt by the budding railway system."*

Another scheme of an independent company that came to nothing was for a line from Cambridge to Thetford. Notice was given in *The London Gazette* of 23 November 1843 of intention to apply for an Act for " The Thetford & Cambridge Railway." The station at Cambridge was to be on the outskirts of the town in Trumpington parish, near the present River Farm.

Meantime an improvement had begun in the affairs of the Northern & Eastern Company. In 1843 an Act was passed authorising the extension of the line from Bishop's Stortford to Newport, and in 1844 a further Act enabled the line to be continued " from Newport by Cambridge to Ely and thence eastward to Brandon and westward to Peterborough." At Brandon the line was to connect at a head-on junction with a railway which was being made from Norwich and Yarmouth. It was under the Act of 1844 that railway communication between London and Cambridge was actually established and the station built where it now stands.† Just previously a working arrangement had been authorised between the Northern & Eastern and Eastern Counties Railways, and as from 1 January 1844 the two companies were to work as one concern. The line from Newport to Cambridge and Brandon was therefore actually constructed by the Eastern Counties Railway. Robert Stephenson was the engineer. This line, including the line from Bishop's Stortford to Newport, was laid down with a 4 ft. 8½ in. gauge, and nearly a year before the opening to Cambridge the original 5 ft. gauge of the line between Bishop's Stortford and London had been altered to standard gauge. At the same time a change was made on the Colchester section, so that the 5 ft. gauge which John Braithwaite had used in constructing the Eastern Counties' original line was completely given up.

* H. G. Lewin, *Early British Railways* (1925), p. 97.

† " An Act to enable the Eastern Counties Railway Company to make a railway from the Northern and Eastern Railway at Newport by Cambridge to Ely and thence eastward to Brandon and westward to Peterborough." (7 and 8 Vict., cap. lxii.)

The formal opening of the railway, with its station near Hills Road at Cambridge, took place on 29 July 1845, and on the following day the public train service began.

The Act of 1844 which authorised the construction of the line to Cambridge had sections giving officers of the University free access at all reasonable times to the Company's station at Cambridge and empowering them to ask for information from the Railway Company's servants regarding any person on the station " who," in the words of the Act, " shall be a member of the University or suspected of being such." Other sections forbade the Company to convey any member of the University not having the degree of Master of Arts or Bachelor of Civil Law or Medicine as a passenger if so requested by a duly authorised officer of the University even if he had paid his fare. The prohibition held good for 24 hours. The Company was also prohibited under penalty of a fine from taking up or setting down any person known to be *in statu pupillari* except at the regular appointed stations. None of these vexatious sections was to be found in the Act of 1836 under which the railway could have been made to Cambridge, but between 1836 and 1844 Oxford had been threatened with a railway and for disciplinary reasons the Oxford University authorities had words introduced into the Great Western's Oxford railway Act of 1843, which were copied practically verbatim in the Act of 1844 under which the construction of the railway to Cambridge was actually authorised.

There was a curious prohibition in the Cambridge railway Act which affected the travelling public generally. Under a penalty of a fine not exceeding £5 for each offence " for the benefit of Addenbrooke's Hospital or other County Charity to be decided by the University," the Company was prohibited from taking up or setting down any passenger at the Cambridge railway station or at any place within 3 miles of the same between 10 a.m. and 5 p.m. on any Sunday.* Parliament, however, was considerate enough to enact that if by some unavoidable

---

* Soon after the opening of the line cheap day tickets were issued on Sundays to Cambridge (7 a.m. from Shoreditch). This drew a protest in 1851 from the Vice-Chancellor of the University. Excursions on Sundays were, he wrote, " as distasteful to the University Authorities as they must be offensive to Almighty God and to all right-minded Christians " (quoted in Arthur Gray, *The Town of Cambridge* (1925), p. 185).

accident a train was late, passengers might alight or join the train during the prohibited hours. This section was not repealed till 1908, though long before that it had become a dead letter.

The station at Cambridge, which was opened with the railway in 1845, was described in the contemporary *Railway Chronicle* as " a long flat and handsome brick building, with stone dressings, consisting of a double series of arcades ; one extending over the siding of the railway and the other serving as a portico for the road carriages arriving at the station . . . its proportions are good ; its architectural expression is rather Palladian, but it has a character arising as all architectural expression ought to do, from its peculiar use, and the idea of accommodating both kinds of traffic under the same roof seems worthy of general attention." There were several contemporary illustrations ; two are reproduced.

The station had one long platform for use by both up and down trains, but after a few years the single platform, then of no great length, was found insufficient for the increasing traffic, and a wooden island platform was built for the up trains. This island platform communicated with the main platform and booking offices by a foot-bridge with steep stairways for the use of passengers, but a tunnel was provided under the line for the transfer of luggage.

In 1863 the station was remodelled. The wooden platform, footbridge, and luggage tunnel were abolished, and all trains, up and down, again used a single platform which, as reconstructed, was 1,200 ft. in length.* In 1886 plans for a completely new double-platform station were prepared, but, as this reconstruction involved taking a piece of Coldham Common for a short section of new line for the Newmarket branch, Parliament would not sanction the proposal, so the scheme for a really fine station was withdrawn.

In 1893 the Company came forward with further plans. This time Parliament sanctioned the taking of a piece of Coldham Common to provide a new junction and easier curve for the Newmarket branch, but, as the general feeling in Cambridge seems to have been in favour of

---

* Details of the structural changes from 1845 to 1863 will be found in *The Railway Magazine*, lxxvii (November 1935), p. 378, contributed mainly by the present writer.

leaving the old station as it was, the Company did not proceed with the reconstruction of the platforms but merely improved the layout of the line to Newmarket. From 1908 onwards there have been many minor improvements such as reconstructing the offices, widening the platform and still further lengthening it to 1,650 ft., but still leaving it a single platform for main line traffic.

The opening of the railway was the occasion of a second attempt to make Cambridge a railway centre. During the Session of 1845 a Bill was promoted in Parliament by an independent company for a line from Cambridge to Lincoln to be connected at Cambridge with the Eastern Counties Railway to London. In the first notices and plans deposited in 1844 the railway was to commence on the south side of Cambridge " in or near Coe Fen " and to be connected with the Eastern Counties' London line near Clay Farm, and passing under the Wimpole Road near the House in the Fields and the St. Neots Road to go to the west of the Observatory on to St. Ives and Lincoln ; but the company amended these proposals and suggested commencing the line at a junction north of the Eastern Counties' Cambridge station and using that station for their traffic. The Cambridge & Lincoln Company's Bill had strong Cambridge support and was recommended to Parliament by the Railway Department of the Board of Trade, not only on its merits as the best scheme for connecting London with Lincoln and eventually with York, but because the route had to a certain extent already received the sanction of the Legislature, since the preamble of the Northern & Eastern Company's Act, passed in 1836, recited " that the making of a railway from London to Cambridge with a view to its being extended hereafter to the northern and eastern counties of England would be of great public advantage."*

Notwithstanding these recommendations, the Bill was thrown out on technical grounds, as some errors in levels were discovered in the plans and sections which had escaped the notice of the Standing Orders Committee.

Another Bill was introduced in this Session, promoted by an independent company but advantageous to the Eastern Counties' Cambridge line—the Tottenham &

* *Reports of the Railway Department of the Board of Trade on Schemes for extending railway communication and amalgamations of railways, Sess. 1845, XII (London and York), para. 86.*

Farringdon Street Extension Bill. The line proposed by this Bill was to commence at a junction with the Eastern Counties' Cambridge line at Tottenham and run to a terminus in Farringdon Street, to be used as an alternative to, and not instead of, the Shoreditch terminus. The proposed line would have reached London by a less circuitous route than *via* Stratford. The Bill was recommended by the Railway Department of the Board of Trade as providing a better terminus for the Cambridge line than " the remote and inconvenient terminus of Shoreditch," but it failed to become law and the project was dropped.

The case was different with the rejected Cambridge & Lincoln Bill ; another Bill for a similar line was immediately promoted, though this time by the Eastern Counties Railway, and was introduced in the Parliamentary Session of 1846 as an extension of their line from Cambridge to Lincoln. This Bill was thrown out by the House of Lords Committee. The line under this Bill was shown as leaving Cambridge on the north side of the town, branching from the Ely line to the left between Mill Road and Coldham Lane. The station used would have been the existing one belonging to the Company, and Cambridge would have become an important station on a trunk line between London and the North.

The Eastern Counties Railway had succeeded in getting Parliamentary sanction for a branch line from Cambridge, just north of the station, to St. Ives, with arrangements to run on to Huntingdon over the line to be made from St. Ives by another Company. The Act was obtained on 8 August 1845, and the line from Cambridge was opened in two years.

But there were many other proposals put forward in 1845-1846 for railways to Cambridge from different parts of England—at least eight definite schemes. A public meeting was held in the Cambridge Town Hall on 19 November 1845, convened by and presided over by the Mayor, at which George Hudson, already known as " the Railway King," was the principal speaker. At this meeting the schemes for the projected railways were outlined. The immediate result was the appointment of a Committee to enquire into the merits of the various proposals and, more particularly, to consider the practicability of establishing a central station in Cambridge.

The Committee presented its report at a public meeting held at the Town Hall on 23 January 1846.*

As to a central station the report ran as follows :

"The Committee . . . beg leave to report as their opinion that under existing circumstances, there does not appear to be any practicable mode of obtaining a general central station at Cambridge but that the convenience of the public would be greatly consulted by an enlargement of the present Eastern Counties station ; public access thereto being afforded by way of East Road near the Town Gaol, *together with the addition of a passenger station near the Town Gaol.*"

In 1846 the Town Gaol was close to Parker's Piece where Queen Anne Terrace now stands. Presumably a station near there would have been reached by a line about three-quarters of a mile in length, curving from the main station. Nothing came of the Committee's proposal.

On the new railways to be made from Cambridge, the Committee reported in favour of :

(i) The extension of the Eastern Counties Railway from its station near Hills Road to Lincoln and York to leave Cambridge on the north of the town ;

(ii) the Wisbeach, St. Ives & Cambridge Junction Railway ;

(iii) the Cambridge & Oxford Railway, provided that the two alternative termini on the north west of St. Peter's College and the approaches thereto be given up, and " that arrangements can be made to introduce the railway into the town so as not to be objectionable to any College " ;

(iv) the Midland & Eastern Counties Railway, from Cambridge by St. Neots to Northampton and on to Worcester ;

(v) the Bedford and Cambridge extension, provided that it does not cross the Trumpington Road with a " level crossing " ; and

(vi) the Bury St. Edmunds & Cambridge Union Extension.

The Committee did not report in favour of the projected " Newmarket & Chesterford with a branch to Cambridge Railway", but the Bill got Parliamentary sanction. This railway was constructed and later became part of the Eastern Counties Railway, giving direct communication between Cambridge and Newmarket, though the section of line from Chesterford to Six Mile Bottom became derelict.†

* *Cambridge Chronicle*, 24 January 1846.

† See Kenneth Brown, *A Derelict Railway : being the history of the Newmarket and Chesterford Railway* (Cambridge Antiquarian Society's Communications, Vol. XXXI ; paper read 14 November 1927).

Of the schemes approved by the Committee three obtained Acts :

(i) The Wisbeach, St. Ives & Cambridge Junction Railway, which was taken over by the Eastern Counties Railway and formed an extension of the already authorised line from Cambridge to St. Ives ;

(ii) the Bedford and Cambridge extension, which was the proposed Eastern Counties Railway's branch line from Shelford to Bedford, of which, however, only 5 miles from the junction with the main line north of Shelford to Shepreth were constructed ; and

(iii) the Cambridge & Oxford Railway, though this scheme was most drastically cut down by Parliament. The Company promoting this line, with its name changed, eventually enabled the Great Northern Railway to get access to Cambridge ; its history is dealt with later.

During the year 1846 the Eastern Counties Railway put forward a proposal to make an additional station in Cambridge, and also to make what would have been for some 35 miles an alternative line to London. The proposed railway was to leave the existing main line near Shelford and to join the Company's existing line at Ware, passing through Royston, Barkway, Buntingford, and Braughing. Notice was given in *The London Gazette* of 14 November 1846 of the Company's intention to apply for an Act for the construction of this line, and also " for a branch railway to be used as a tram road commencing at or near the bridge by means of which the Hills Road passes over the Eastern Counties Railway and terminating at a common in the parish of Little St. Mary otherwise St. Mary the Less in the borough of Cambridge, the property of the Mayor Aldermen and Burgesses of the borough of Cambridge."

This branch line was to leave the main line south of Cambridge station and run with a curve behind Brookland's Farm, across Trumpington Road over Coe Fen and Sheeps Green to terminate at the north end of Sheeps Green at the river Cam. It would have been about 1¾ miles in length. From the plan showing the layout of the junction it appears that the branch was intended for a shuttle service.* The proposal to make this branch was dropped by the Company, perhaps at the request of the University authorities, and it may be that this was the scheme referred to by Mr. Alderman Akins at a meeting of the Town Council on 15 December 1863, when he said, " The Great Eastern Railway had in the past proposed a central station in Cambridge but the University had opposed it."†

The company proceeded with the Bill for the line from Shelford to Ware, and it was passed by the House of Commons in 1847, but, with several other railways' Bills, it was suspended until the following Session, when it was thrown out as not complying with Standing Orders, and the Company abandoned the scheme. The route of the proposed line was practically the same as in John and George Rennie's plan of 1825 and in Joseph Gibbs' revised plan of 1841.

* A copy of the deposited plan is preserved in the Map Room of the University Library, Cambridge, and is entitled " Town of Cambridge. Proposed branch to the river Cam " (Maps 53.2, 84.6).

† *Cambridge Chronicle*, 19 December 1863.

(Photo: Locomotive & General Railway Photographs)

L.M.S. Cambridge train on the single line near Sandy in 1927; "Precursor" class locomotive 5249 Bellerophon

III	*The Cambridge & Oxford Railway Bill*, 1846,
	and its Sequel

THE promoters of the Cambridge & Oxford Railway deposited their Bill for the Parliamentary Session of 1846. It had a certain amount of support from both Universities. A general committee which had been formed to further the scheme included at the Cambridge end the Vice-Chancellor, the Master of Corpus Christi College, and many Fellows and Tutors of Colleges, while Oxford was represented by several Heads of Colleges and Officers of the University. The line had been surveyed by an eminent engineer, Joseph Locke ; it was 73 miles in length but was a single line throughout. The deposited plan shows four sites, alternatives, for the terminus in Cambridge* :

   (i) Opposite the new Botanic Garden but on the west side of Trumpington Road on land adjoining that road ;

 (ii) Between Little St. Mary Lane and Mill Lane, near the river ;

(iii) Approximately where Queen's Road and Sidgwick Avenue now (1948) meet ;

(iv) The use of the Eastern Counties' station, opened in 1845, a few months before the Bill was deposited.

When the Bill was before Parliament the promoters, however, asked only for the use of the existing station and a junction with the Eastern Counties line close to Hills Road Bridge, just outside the station. The route to Oxford was through Royston, Hitchin, Luton, Dunstable, Cheddington, Aylesbury, and Thame. The Bill passed the House of Commons, but in the House of Lords it was drastically amended and cut down from 73 to 13 miles. The railway actually authorised was only between Hitchin and Royston, but it was stipulated that it should be laid with a double line of rails. The title of the Bill was

* A copy of the deposited plan, " County of Cambridge, Sheet 1," showing the sites is kept in the Cambridge University Library, Map Room (Maps bb.36.84.7).

changed to agree with the facts, and the Cambridge & Oxford Railway Bill received the Royal Assent on 16 July 1846 as The Royston & Hitchin Railway Act.

As soon as this Act was passed, the Great Northern Railway (the main line from Peterborough to King's Cross was then being built) agreed to take a lease of the Royston & Hitchin Railway, such lease to come into operation on 1 August 1850, in the hope that Parliament would sanction an extension of the line from Royston to Cambridge by that date.

In 1847 a Bill was introduced to authorise this lease or for the purchase of the line by the Great Northern, also for the extension of the line from Royston through Shepreth, Barrington, Haslingfield, and Grantchester to Cambridge, where the terminus was to be on a plot of land adjoining the south side of the new Botanic Garden ground, lying between this and the north side of the road or avenue leading to and from Brookland House in the parish of St. Andrew-the-Less, with a spur line from the railway in the parish of Trumpington to join the Eastern Counties Railway about 235 yards south of the Hills Road Bridge for exchange of traffic. Parliament agreed to the Great Northern Railway taking a lease of the Royston & Hitchin line but would not sanction the extension to Cambridge.

In 1848 another Bill was introduced for a similar extension from Royston through Shepreth to Cambridge, but with the terminus north-east of the Botanic Garden on vacant land bounded on the north by Russell Street and on the east by Hills Road, with a spur line to the Eastern Counties Railway for exchange of traffic. The Bill contained a proposal to make a branch at Shepreth to join the line which the Eastern Counties Railway had in 1847 been authorised to make from their main line near Shelford to Bedford through Shepreth.*

Parliament refused to sanction the extension of the Royston & Hitchin line to Cambridge but agreed to an extension as far as Shepreth and also to a junction there with the Eastern Counties line when constructed. Section 13 of this Act (11 and 12 Vict. c. cxix) enacted that the

---

* This line to Bedford was never made, but, under pressure, the Eastern Counties Railway constructed about 5 miles of it from Shelford junction to Shepreth. The railway from Cambridge to Bedford, opened in 1862 and worked by the London & North Western Railway, was a different undertaking.

extension " shall commence in the parish of Bassingbourn in the said county of Cambridge by a junction with the authorised line of the Royston & Hitchin Railway and shall terminate by a junction with the Cambridge & Bedford Railway in the parish of Shepreth." This provision in the Act was intended to secure access to Cambridge for trains from King's Cross when the Great Northern main line through Hitchin was completed. Running powers over the Eastern Counties' rails were not expressly given, and, doubtless by inadvertence, the usual words were omitted giving the right to use water tanks, stations, etc.* The Royston & Hitchin Company therefore continued to promote Bills for an independent line to Cambridge with a terminus of its own.

However in 1850 a Bill was introduced by an independent company—though doubtless supported by the Great Northern Railway—to make a line direct from Shepreth to Cambridge through Barrington and Haslingfield with a terminus on land adjoining the Botanic Gardens and a connecting spur line, as in the previous Bills, to the Eastern Counties Railway outside Cambridge. The Mayor and Corporation and a number of the inhabitants petitioned Parliament in favour of it. The promotion of this Bill had strong local support, as shown by a meeting which was held on 24 December 1849, presided over by the Mayor, urging the importance of a separate line from Shepreth to be quite independent of the Eastern Counties Railway. The University Members opposed the Bill in the House on the grounds that it would be very inconvenient to have two separate stations in the town, and also because the proposed line and terminus would take land intended for an extension of the Botanic Garden. The Bill (known as the Cambridge & Shepreth Junction Railway Bill) was thrown out.

In 1851 the Bill was again introduced but was withdrawn. In the same session, however, the Royston & Hitchin Company introduced a Bill for an extension from Shepreth through Barrington and Grantchester to a terminus on land adjoining Silver Street in St. Botolph's parish, with a spur to the Eastern Counties Railway, and a line branching off at Trumpington to join the Cambridge branch of the Newmarket & Chesterford Railway near

* Bradshaw's *Railway Shareholders' Manual* for 1852, p. 71.

Pole Cat Farm. (The Newmarket & Chesterford Railway had not at that date been purchased by the Eastern Counties Railway.) This Bill for a direct line from Shepreth to Cambridge was opposed by the Eastern Counties Railway as a competing line from Cambridge to London, to enable the Great Northern Railway to run through trains *via* Hitchin to their terminus at King's Cross, which had been recently opened.

The Bill was opposed by the University Members in Parliament on the grounds that the railway would pass " under the windows of St. Peter's College and at the back of the University, and also because a second station in the Town was undesirable." The Bill was thrown out.

But the Great Northern had on 1 August 1851 completed the line from Royston to Shepreth as authorised by the Act of 1848.* Being determined to get traffic to Cambridge somehow they opened an office in Trinity Street and for some months ran a service of four-horse omnibuses to connect with the King's Cross trains at Shepreth, with through bookings, road and rail, from Cambridge. This did not pay, so in the following year, 1852, when the Eastern Counties Railway had made their line from Shelford to Shepreth (a single line), the Great Northern granted a lease of the Shepreth-Hitchin line to the Eastern Counties Railway for 14 years. A head-on junction was put in at Shepreth, thus completing rail communications between Cambridge and Hitchin, and the Eastern Counties worked with their own locomotives and carriages a local service between Cambridge and Hitchin. At first three, and later, four trains ran each way on week-days and two on Sundays for 14 years.

The lease of the Great Northern line from Shepreth to Hitchin granted to the Eastern Counties was only for 14 years ; therefore on 1 April 1866 the Great Northern would resume occupation of it, but this would only enable them to get from King's Cross to Shepreth. Full running powers over the Eastern Counties line from Shepreth would be required to work traffic to Cambridge. With this in view the Great Northern made another attempt— this time successful—to get access to Cambridge. The

---

* The Royston & Hitchin Railway, Shepreth Extension Act 1848 (11 and 12 Vict., c. cxix) ; and as from 1 August 1850 the Royston & Hitchin undertaking had been leased in perpetuity to the Great Northern Company.

proposal was to make use of a section of the London & North Western Company's new Bedford and Cambridge line, or, alternatively, to use the Eastern Counties, now called the Great Eastern, line from Shepreth, but under both plans to go to an independent terminus near the centre of Cambridge.

On 1 August 1862 the Bedford and Cambridge line had been opened to Cambridge. It joined the Great Eastern Railway just south of Hills Road bridge and used that company's station. Although the line was made by a local company, the directors being Bedfordshire and Cambridgeshire men, it was worked and very soon purchased by the London & North Western Railway. At that time the Great Northern Railway was on very friendly terms with the North Western, so for the Parliamentary Session of 1864 the Great Northern promoted a Bill to extend the Royston & Hitchin line from Shepreth through Barrington and Haslingfield to join the London & North Western line about 1½ miles on the Cambridge side of Lord's Bridge Station, to double the line from that point to Cambridge, and to use it for their trains to the outskirts of the town. The Great Northern also sought powers to make a station on a site bounded by Orchard Street and Emmanuel Road close to Christ's Pieces as their Cambridge terminus ; this was to be reached by a new line, just under 2 miles long and running chiefly in a cutting, which was to branch off from the London & North Western line a short distance south of the existing Cambridge station.

The new line, when in a cutting, would have been crossed at Brooklands Avenue, Hills Road, Station Road, and Mill Road by bridges carrying those roads over the railway at the existing road levels. In this way the Great Northern could have run trains between King's Cross and their new terminus in Emmanuel Road without touching the Great Eastern Railway.

The Bill had an alternative scheme—for the Great Northern to have full running powers and the use of stations from Shepreth to Cambridge over the Great Eastern line and through Cambridge station to a point just beyond Mill Road, where the Great Northern would make their own line curving to the left and running between the Workhouse and the Cemetery to the new terminus in Emmanuel Road. The line would be under a mile in length. By this route the Great Northern would not be independent of the Great Eastern but would have statutory rights to use their line, stations, etc.

The Bill was supported by the Cambridge Borough Council and by the Board of Improvement Commissioners, with a general preference to the new terminus being approached by the alternative route, *i.e.* through the existing station as better for exchange of traffic. Objection was raised by the then Master of Christ's College to a goods and coal depot being attached to the terminus in Emmanuel Road. In his opinion both Christ's and Emmanuel Colleges would become almost uninhabitable by the continual howling and whistling of the engines. His objection was supported by the Vice-Chancellor, so the Great Northern agreed to have the goods station to the east of Clarendon Street.

The Great Eastern opposed the Bill in Parliament, but a last-minute compromise was arrived at. The Great Eastern agreed to give the Great Northern effectual running powers over their lines between Shepreth and Cambridge, with the use of all the stations, and to provide the Great Northern with a separate booking office and platform at Cambridge and accommodation for their engines, etc. The Great Eastern also agreed to double the branch line to Shepreth and to make it a line fit for express traffic before 31 March 1866. The Great Northern for its part agreed to withdraw the proposal for a central station in Cambridge and also the proposal for making the independent line from Shepreth. An Agreement settling the matter was sanctioned by Parliament in 1864 and was embodied in an Act (27 and 28 Vict. cap. cxxiv). The Royston & Hitchin Company continued in existence until July 1897, when it was vested in the Great Northern.

Owing to shortage of money the Great Eastern did not double the Shepreth branch by the agreed date, but did so about a year afterwards ; on 1 April, 1866, however, the Great Northern began the through service between Cambridge and King's Cross, notwithstanding the 5 miles of single road ; the distance was just under 58 miles.

No further attempt was made by any company to make a second and more central station in Cambridge.

IV   *Cambridge a Railway Centre*, 1866 *and After*

B Y April 1866 when the Great Northern Company began to exercise running powers into the station, Cambridge had become a railway centre, with trains of four separate companies using the station—G.E., G.N., L.&N.W., and Midland Railways—converging on Cambridge from north, south, east, and west:

From the north—

From Norwich	.	1845	G.E.R.
,, St. Ives and Huntingdon	.	1847	G.E.R.
,, Peterborough *via* Ely	.	1847	G.E.R.
,, Kettering (Midland Railway) *via* Huntingdon (*with running powers*)	.	1866	M.R.

From the south—

From London *via* Bishop's Stortford	.	1845	G.E.R.
,, Colchester and Haverhill *via* Shelford*	.	1865	G.E.R.
,, London *via* Hitchin (Great Northern) *with running powers*	.	1866	G.N.R.

From the east—

From Newmarket	.	1851	G.E.R.
,, Bury St. Edmunds (extension from Newmarket)	.	1854	G.E.R.

From the west—

From Bedford, Bletchley, and Oxford (L.N.W.R.) *with running powers*	.	1862	L.N.W.R.

* It may be mentioned that as early as 1845 two independent companies—the Cambridge & Colchester Junction Railway and the Colchester & Cambridge Direct Railway—had put forward schemes for connecting Colchester with Cambridge, but neither got beyond preliminary proceedings.

Since 1866 there have been a few additions :

(i) *St. Pancras :* through carriages, and later through trains, to and from St. Pancras, Midland Railway, *via* the Tottenham and Hampstead Junction Railway from July 1870 (Great Eastern coaches and engines being used) ;　　　　　(G.E.R.)

(ii) *Fordham :* a new line from Fordham joining at Barnwell Junction in 1884 ;　　　　　(G.E.R.)

(iii) *Doncaster and Lincoln :* through expresses between Doncaster and Liverpool Street in 1883 (by G.N. and G.E. Joint line through Lincoln) with the service extended to York some 10 years later ;　　　　　(G.E.R.)

(iv) Better Newmarket approach line : a new and easier approach for the Newmarket trains by a new line over part of Coldham Common in 1896.　(G.E.R.)

(Photo: Locomotive & General Railway Photographs)

Cambridge Station from the south end in the nineteen-thirties: the late G.N.R. and L.N.W.R. bays to left, main platform to right

APPENDIX

SOME NOTES ON PASSENGER ENGINES WORKING INTO CAMBRIDGE

I   Eastern Counties Railway and Great Eastern Railway

In 1845, when the railway reached Cambridge, Stothert & Slaughter built ten express engines of the 2-2-2 type, with 6 ft. driving wheels, for the E.C.R. and in 1846 seven more ; in 1847 five more of the same class were built by E. B. Wilson & Co. These engines probably worked the 5 p.m. non-stop train from Bishopsgate to Cambridge in 1852.

In 1862 to 1867 Robert Sinclair's 2-2-2 engines with outside cylinders and 7 ft. driving wheels appeared. Thirty-one were built, some by the French firm of Schneider at Le Creusot, but one was destroyed in the Thorpe collision in 1874. The late E. L. Ahrons regarded these as the most celebrated of the Eastern Counties and Great Eastern engines. They did practically all the main-line express work for many years.

In 1874 two express engines, Nos. 301 and 302, were built at Stratford, designed by S. W. Johnson but completed after he had left to take charge of the Midland Railway's locomotives. They were 6 ft. 7 in. 4-4-0, used much on the St. Pancras and Cambridge expresses.

In 1879 Massey Bromley designed some 7 ft. 6 in. 4-2-2 engines. Twenty were built, Nos. 245-254 by Dübs & Co. in 1879 and Nos. 600-609 by Kitson & Co. in 1881-1882. Ahrons wrote that "the way they used to climb the Bethnal Green bank was astonishing ".*

In 1884 and 1885 T. W. Worsdell's two-cylinder compound 7 ft. 4-4-0 appeared, eleven in all. Until converted from compound to simple engines in 1892, they were all stationed at Stratford for express traffic on both sections of the Great Eastern system.

From 1886 to 1897 James Holden's 7 ft. 2-4-0 of the 710 class was built at Stratford, becoming the standard G.E.R. express engine. *Petrolea*, one of this class, used liquid fuel. Ahrons considered the performances of the 710 class to be good but not brilliant. They usually kept very good time without having to run at exceptional speeds. J. Holden also built twenty-one 7 ft. 2-2-2 in 1889 to 1893.

In 1900 J. Holden's *Claud Hamilton*, 7 ft. 4-4-0, appeared, known from number and year of building as the 1900 class.

In 1911 Stephen Holden's 6 ft. 6 in. 4-6-0 No. 1500, first of a class of eighty-nine engines, was built.

In 1928, L.N.E.R. No. 2800 *Sandringham*, the first of Sir Nigel Gresley's three-cylinder 6 ft. 8 in. 4-6-0, was built.

---

* "Locomotive and Train Working in the Latter Part of the Nineteenth Century," Great Eastern Railway, *The Railway Magazine*, xlii (1918), p. 152.

II Great Northern Railway

When the Great Northern first ran its own trains into Cambridge in 1866, 2-2-2 tank engines built by Sharp Brothers of Manchester in 1852 were used, and perhaps some of the original " Little Sharps " —tender engines of an earlier date but converted to tank engines in that year—were also among those used for the express passenger trains.

Some information regarding the type of engine used is given in the Board of Trade Report on a derailment which took place near Royston on 3 July 1866.* Archibald Sturrock was still in charge at Doncaster till the end of 1866.

Between 1868 and 1870 Patrick Stirling's 7 ft. 1 in. 2-2-2 express engines were built—twelve in all—and in later years frequently worked the Cambridge expresses.

Rebuilds of Sturrock's engines were also used, notably, according to Ahrons, the 7 ft. 2-4-0, two of which were rebuilt by Stirling in 1873 and four more later, all as 2-2-2s. Engines of this class, as rebuilt, were in the late 1870's in general use on the Cambridge expresses. Some of Sturrock's 6 ft. 2-4-0s were also rebuilt, but as 2-4-0s, and were, in my recollection, in use on the Cambridge line in the 1880's.

In 1883 and 1884 Kitson & Co., of Leeds, built fifteen 2-4-0s, 6 ft. 7½ in. driving wheels, Nos. 701-715, much used on the Cambridge line in my recollection.

In 1885 the first of Stirling's 7 ft. 7½ in. 2-2-2 was built. This class was much used later on Cambridge expresses.

Another notable class that worked on the Cambridge line about 1904 was H. A. Ivatt's rebuild, with steam dome, of Stirling's famous 8 ft. 1 in. 4-2-2. Ivatt's " Atlantics " of 1898 and 1902 also worked the Cambridge expresses in later years.

III London & North Western Railway

Among the many classes of engines used on the Bletchley and Cambridge branch were the 6 ft. 6 in. 2-2-2 locomotives built in 1858-1861, known as the " Small Bloomers." These were used at first for main-line traffic, but many were later transferred to branch lines until they were scrapped in the early 1880's.

John Ramsbottom's 6 ft. coupled engines known as the " Samson " class, built in 1863, with the ten built by F. W. Webb in the 1870's, were also used for the Cambridge traffic, and at a later date some of the famous " Lady of the Lake " class 7 ft. 7½ in. 2-2-2 were also to be seen on this branch. *Daphne* of this class, built in 1865, No. 1433, worked on the branch in 1903.

Daphne (according to information obtained by the late E. L. Ahrons†) bore a very good reputation amongst the engine-men, and was said to be the only one of the type which could really be relied upon to work trains on the Cambridge branch, a rather " tricky " line with the Gamlingay bank going down and the adverse gradient coming up from Bedford to Ridgmont.

---

* See *The Railway Magazine*, xcii (1946), pp. 216 and 322.

† *The Railway Magazine*, xxxvii (1915), p. 383.

IV   Midland Railway

In his series of articles in *The Railway Magazine** on " Locomotive and Train Working in the Latter Part of the Nineteenth Century," the late E. L. Ahrons, in dealing with the Midland Company's Cambridge trains, stated that for many years engine No. 239 was the usual Midland representative stabled at Cambridge. This engine was one of ten—the 230 class—built by Beyer Peacock & Co. in 1868 as 2-4-0 side tanks but converted to tender engines in 1870. They had coupled driving wheels 6 ft. 2½ in. (approximately).   Two other engines of this class were at Kettering shed.

At a later date trains between Kettering and Cambridge were worked by engines of the 1070 class, designed by M. Kirtley and built by Sharp Stewart & Co. in 1874 ; these were 2-4-0, coupled wheels 6 ft. 6½ in., and were all rebuilt in 1887-1890.   Mr. Ahrons states that one of this class was stabled at Cambridge about 1919. He also says that " at one time the Nottingham engines Nos. 2, 5, and 12 had a turn through to Cambridge," but some years prior to 1919.   These engines were of the 890 class 2-4-0, coupled wheels 6 ft. 8½ in., designed by M. Kirtley and built at Derby in 1872-1874.

Further particulars of the classes of engines working passenger trains into Cambridge over the lines of the constituent companies forming the L.M.S. and L.N.E.R. groups will be found in Mr. S. P. W. Corbett's interesting article " Cambridge as a Railway Centre," published in *The Railway Magazine* of December 1934, Vol. lxxv, p. 422 ; and also in three articles entitled " Cambridge Memories, 1925-45," by Mr. D. A. Beacock, which appeared as recently as March, April, and May 1947, in *Railways*.   Both are fully illustrated, and Mr. Corbett's article includes a map showing the railways in the Cambridge area.

---

* *The Railway Magazine*, xliv (1919), p. 390, xlv (1919), p. 344.